The
FIRST MOON LANDING

RROOOAAARRR!

"Lift-off! We have lift-off!"

It is 16th July 1969, and America's historic *Apollo 11* is soaring into clear blue Florida skies. Its destination – the Moon. Soon men will walk on another world for the very first time.

People have always been fascinated by the Moon. Long ago, they worshipped it as a god or goddess. Many noticed how the Moon changed shape, from a tiny slither to a full circle and back again. They named the time this took a "month".

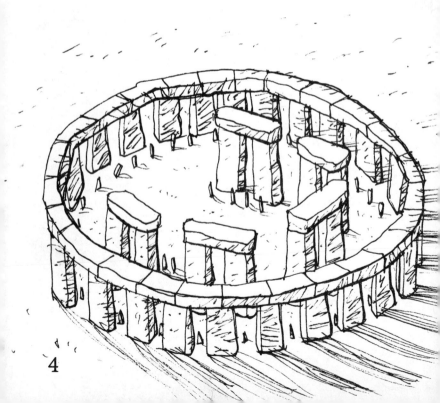

Later astronomers found a new way to study the Moon. In 1610, Galileo used a telescope to look at it – and he saw mountains and craters! Before this, everyone had thought the Moon was perfectly smooth. Galileo made fine drawings of his discoveries.

Men and women dreamed of travelling to the Moon. But how would they get there? In 1865, Jules Verne wrote a book about it, *From the Earth to the Moon.* In it a spaceship was launched from Florida, reached the Moon and splashed down into an ocean on its return. But no one thought Verne's story would come true.

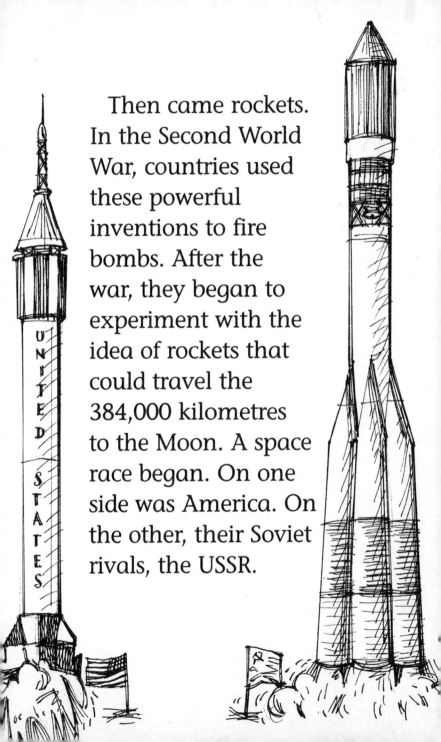

Then came rockets. In the Second World War, countries used these powerful inventions to fire bombs. After the war, they began to experiment with the idea of rockets that could travel the 384,000 kilometres to the Moon. A space race began. On one side was America. On the other, their Soviet rivals, the USSR.

Both countries began their Moon explorations with small unmanned spacecraft. There were more disasters than successes, but scientists discovered a lot about the Moon. They found it has a "dark side" that always faces away from Earth; and its craters and mountains are broken up by dry seas – of ancient and solid volcanic lava, not water.

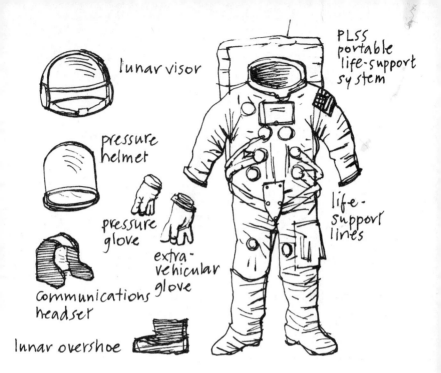

lunar visor

PLSS portable life-support system

pressure helmet

pressure glove

extra-vehicular glove

life-support lines

communications headset

lunar overshoe

Gravity, the force which pulls us to the ground, is much less on the Moon, and there is no air to breathe. And the temperatures can be so hot people will fry, or so cold that they will freeze! So scientists had to design spacesuits to help astronauts stay alive on the Moon.

In August 1961, a man soared
into space at last! After many
practice missions by the USSR and
America, a 27-year-old Soviet
cosmonaut, Yuri Gagarin, reached
orbit. In less than two hours he
had circled the world once, and
returned to Earth. The USSR had
pulled ahead in the space race.

America reacted by giving 25 billion dollars to its space agency, NASA. Surely its new "Project Apollo" would succeed!

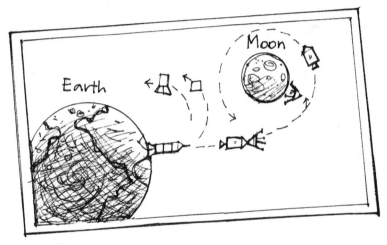

But there were so many problems, and mistakes could be deadly. US scientists decided they would need two spacecraft: one to circle above the Moon while another landed on it. Everything would need to be tested in Earth orbit first.

John Glenn First American to orbit Earth

First Moon-close-up

NASA

American and Soviet missions were advancing year by year... the first US-manned orbit, the first pictures of the Moon, then the first ever spacewalk – by the Russian Alexei Leonov.

Alexei Leonov

CCCP

12

In March 1965, millions of Americans saw their own astronauts orbit Earth and do practice moves in the *Gemini 3* spacecraft. These were important preparations for future Moon missions.

Gemini3 orbit change

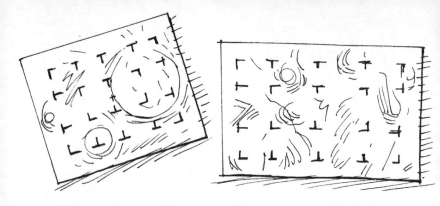

The US scientists were pleased. The *Gemini* and *Apollo* practice missions – in Earth and Moon orbits – had been declared safe and successful. Now the scientists studied pictures of the Moon to find the best landing sites.

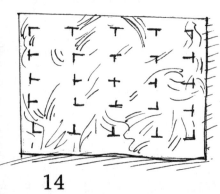

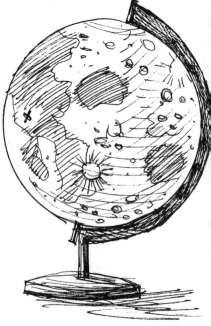

By 14th July 1969, a three day countdown began. At the end of it the *Apollo 11* mission would be launched into space, its destination – the Moon. America hoped it was finally going to beat the Soviets!

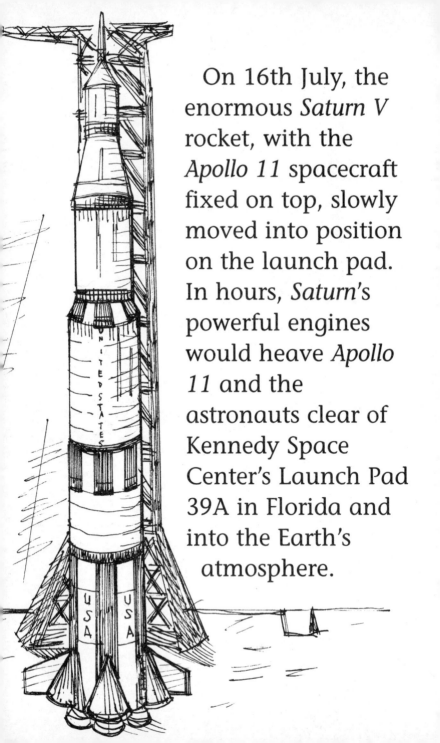

On 16th July, the enormous *Saturn V* rocket, with the *Apollo 11* spacecraft fixed on top, slowly moved into position on the launch pad. In hours, *Saturn's* powerful engines would heave *Apollo 11* and the astronauts clear of Kennedy Space Center's Launch Pad 39A in Florida and into the Earth's atmosphere.

The three astronauts – *Apollo 11*'s Flight Crew – awoke before dawn. Neil Armstrong, Edwin "Buzz" Aldrin and Michael Collins were trained and ready for their historic mission.

Every minute was carefully planned: breakfast, a doctor's examination, getting into spacesuits. At 6.30 a.m. the three men began the drive to the launch pad.

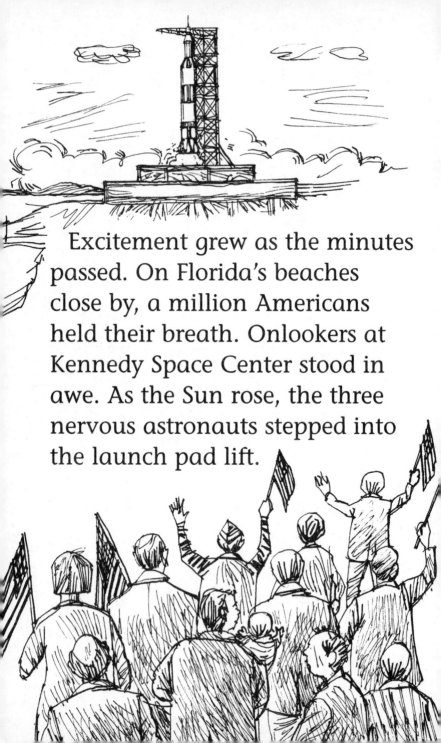

Excitement grew as the minutes passed. On Florida's beaches close by, a million Americans held their breath. Onlookers at Kennedy Space Center stood in awe. As the Sun rose, the three nervous astronauts stepped into the launch pad lift.

At last the three astronauts strapped themselves into *Apollo 11*'s Command Module, on top of the towering *Saturn V* rocket. At 7.30 a.m. the checks began.

At 7.52 a.m. NASA technicians closed the hatch. Five minutes to go. "Happy journey!" radioed Mission Control in Houston, Texas. *Saturn V*'s computer took control of the launch.

Ten seconds. Nine, the start up began. A spray of water cooled the launch pad... Eight, seven, six, five, four, three... Now *Saturn's* engines fired at 100 per cent thrust... Two... flames, and clouds spurted from the rocket's base... One, zero! "LIFT-OFF! We have lift off!" The Moon voyagers roared away at 9.32 a.m.

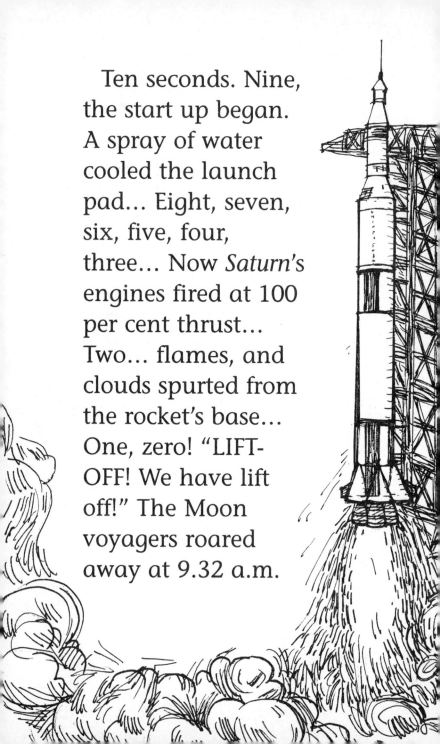

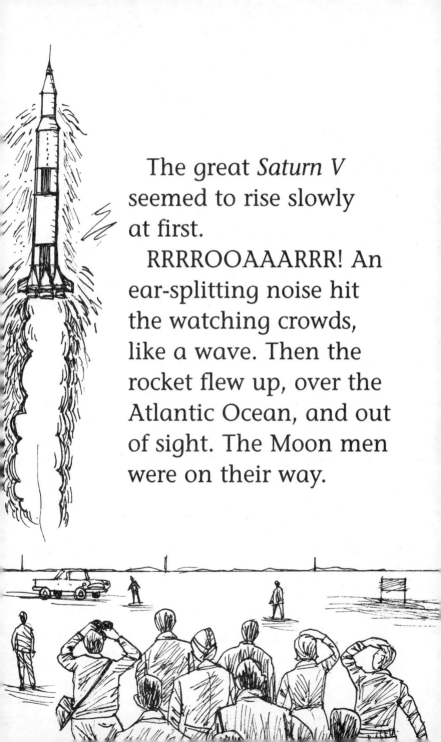

The great *Saturn V* seemed to rise slowly at first.

RRRROOAAARRR! An ear-splitting noise hit the watching crowds, like a wave. Then the rocket flew up, over the Atlantic Ocean, and out of sight. The Moon men were on their way.

The adventure was just beginning. *Saturn*'s rocket had three sections or "stages", and each had to fire perfectly. Stage one lifted the rocket into space. Its fuel used up, this stage was discarded.

By the time stage two was used up, the astronauts were 183 kilometres above the Earth and accelerating. Stage three fired. *Apollo 11* soared into Earth's orbit!

Now *Apollo 11* consisted of the Command Module, the Service Module and the Lunar Module.

With the rocket fuel used up, Michael Collins carefully flew the Command Module away from the rocket.

Then he turned his Module back towards the rocket in order to dock with the Lunar Module, the *Eagle*, stored inside it.

For four days, *Apollo 11* hurtled towards the Moon. It was a journey into the unknown. TV cameras kept Earth and the crewmen in contact.

At last, through their windows, they saw the magnificent grey Moon loom into view.

In less than an hour,
Apollo 11 swung round
behind the Moon – to
the dark side never
seen from Earth.

Engines fired into
life, and slowed
the spacecraft
down to slot into
a Moon, or lunar
orbit.

It was 20th July,
1969, an historic
date. "The Moon
looks like the
pictures," said
Armstrong. "But
there's no substitute
for actually being here."

Now it was time
for Armstrong and
Aldrin to move into
the Lunar Module
Eagle.

Again, *Apollo 11*
swung round to the dark side of
the Moon, out of contact with
Mission Control. The *Eagle* began
to separate from the Command
Module. "The Eagle has
wings... looking good!"
said Armstrong.
The two spacecraft
swung back, to
the visible,
front side, of
the Moon.

Michael Collins steered the Command Module into a higher orbit, where he would wait for his companions to rejoin him in a day or so – after the Moon landing.

Armstrong and Aldrin checked the *Eagle*'s engines. If anything went wrong now, the whole mission would fail.

Eagle disappeared behind the Moon once more. Its engines moved it into a lower position. The lunar craft re-fired its engines, and the descent began. They flew towards the Sea of Tranquillity – their chosen landing spot. "We have visual, Houston," confirmed Armstrong.

Just a few minutes to go to a
Moon landing. This was the final
phase. *Eagle* was vertical now.
Armstrong could see the Moon
below, rushing towards him.
"THERE'S A CRATER RIGHT
BELOW!" he cried. He snatched
the landing controls from the
computers.

The fuel was low. *Eagle* had to land in 60 seconds or the mission would fail! It hovered 23 metres above the Moon. Clouds of Moon dust, disturbed by the engines, blocked Armstrong's view. "Picking up some dust!" he said. Time was running out...

Armstrong made sure *Eagle* was vertical. "Contact light," said Aldrin, nervous but excited. "OK... engine stop... descent engine command override, off... engine arm, off. 413 is in." Then silence. Finally Armstrong spoke four historic words to Houston Control:

"THE *EAGLE* HAS LANDED!"

On Earth, millions sat by their TVs and radios, hardly daring to move. The impossible had happened... men had landed on the Moon! At Mission Control, scientists shouted with joy. America had put a man on the Moon!

Armstrong and Aldrin stepped into their Moon spacesuits.

Carefully crawling on his hands and knees, Armstrong backed out of *Eagle*'s tiny hatch. Slowly he began his climb down the ladder. Spacecraft cameras broadcast his progress to the world.

Now Armstrong stood on the pad at the base of one of *Eagle*'s legs. He took a step, his right boot disturbing the Moon dust.

At last he spoke: "That's one small step for man, one giant leap for mankind!"

Then he took a sample of Moon dust from his boot.

Aldrin climbed down too. "Magnificent desolation," he exclaimed. Then the astronauts set to work. They had just two hours to complete their tasks. Moving in hops, Armstrong and Aldrin fixed a TV camera and tripod near their spacecraft, and began their scientific experiments.

35

They set up equipment, including a Laser Ranging Retro Reflector. It was pointed towards Earth, and it picked up laser beams projected from Earth ground stations. Scientists could tell how far the Moon was from Earth to the nearest 15 centimetres!

Armstrong and Aldrin completed their experiments.

Then they unveiled a plaque: "Here men from the planet Earth first set foot upon the Moon, July 1969, AD. We came in peace for all mankind."

They raised an American flag too, and spoke to President Richard Nixon down on Earth.

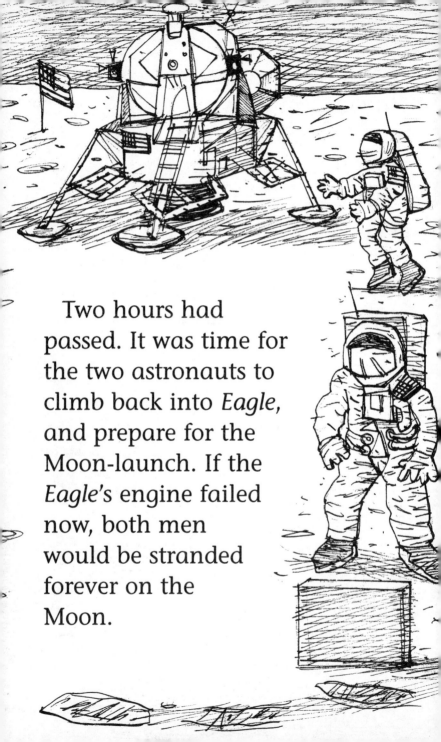

Two hours had passed. It was time for the two astronauts to climb back into *Eagle*, and prepare for the Moon-launch. If the *Eagle*'s engine failed now, both men would be stranded forever on the Moon.

Aldrin and Armstrong did a check. Then Mission Control announced, "You're clear for take-off." "Roger," replied Aldrin.

Eagle's engine burst into life, sending the ascent stage into the blackness above. Behind them on the Moon, they left the flag and plaque, *Eagle*'s landing engine – and their footprints.

Way overhead, Collins was orbiting in the Command Module. Aldrin steered the lunar craft up to dock with it. He had practised this many times before. Then two relieved moonwalkers quickly moved themselves and their Moon souvenirs from the *Eagle* and it was discarded.

VROOSH! The Command
Module fired its engines and sent
the astronauts out of lunar orbit –
and, at 38,616 kmph, hurtling
home to Earth.

Most of the Command Module
could be cast off now. Only
the tiny protective capsule
would be needed,
when the astronauts
hit Earth's
atmosphere.

The engines fired, and the capsule turned. Its vital heatshield withstood the fiery temperatures of re-entry, caused by friction from Earth's atmosphere. Communications blacked out in the heat. The silence was terrible. Then huge parachutes unfurled, to check the capsule's fall.

SPLASSSHH! 195 hours after their lift-off in Florida, the three heroes were home at last, bobbing in the choppy Pacific Ocean! Navy frogmen opened the capsule's hatch, and threw in biological isolation suits. In minutes the astronauts, freshly dressed, were winched into a helicopter and set down safely on a Navy ship.

On land in Houston, the *Apollo* crew settled into the Lunar Receiving Laboratory – their home for the next three weeks. If the astronauts had brought back deadly Moon microbes, they needed to be found! President Nixon greeted Armstrong, Aldrin and Collins through the laboratory window.

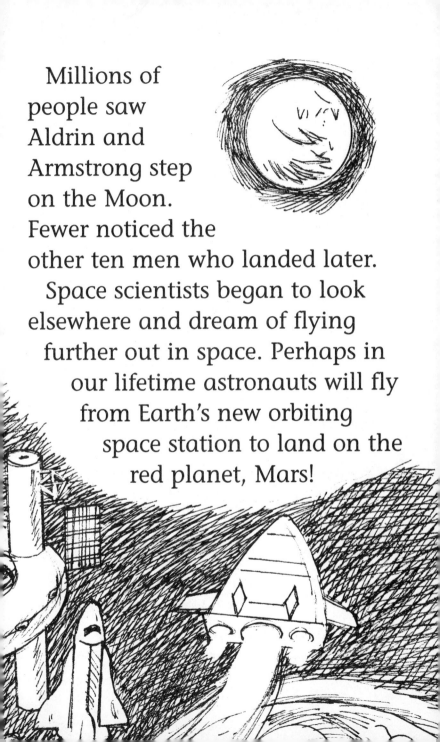

Millions of
people saw
Aldrin and
Armstrong step
on the Moon.
Fewer noticed the
other ten men who landed later.
Space scientists began to look
elsewhere and dream of flying
further out in space. Perhaps in
our lifetime astronauts will fly
from Earth's new orbiting
space station to land on the
red planet, Mars!

Timeline

1920s Oberth in Germany, and Goddard in America study rocket science.

1930s Germany and the USSR experiment with rockets as bomb carriers.

1950s America begins its early rocket programmes. NASA takes over from military scientists.

1958-1959 US's *Pioneer* Moon programme.

1959-1966 USSR's *Luna* programme. *Luna 1* flies by the Moon, *Luna 2* crashes, *Luna 3* photographs its far side.

1961 Yuri Gagarin becomes Russia's first man in space.

1962 John Glenn becomes America's first spaceman in orbit.

1962-65 US's *Ranger* Moon programme.

1965-70 USSR's *Zond* Moon programme.

1966 USSR's *Luna 9* lands on the Moon, *Luna 10*, *11*, and *12* orbit the Moon, *Luna 13* lands on the Moon.

1967 US's *Surveyor 6* lands on the Moon.

May 1969 *Apollo 10* flies by the Moon, and tests the lunar lander module.

July 1969 *Apollo 11* lands the first astronauts on the Moon.

1969 *Apollo 12* lands on the Moon.

1970 An explosion prevents *Apollo 13* from landing on the Moon but it returns safely to Earth.

1970 The USSR send the *Lunakhod* to the Moon. In 1971 this Moon rover explores the Moon.

1971 *Apollo 14* lands on the Moon. *Apollo 15* astronauts explore the Moon's surface in the lunar rover.

1972 *Apollo 16* and *17* land the last men on the Moon.

1986-95 Construction in space of *Mir* space station.

1995 International Space Agencies (US, Canada, Japan, the European Space Agency and Russia) decide to build a space station.

1996 NASA sends missions to Mars.

2000 The first crew go aboard the International Space Station.

2003 European Space Agency's *Beagle 2* lander will look for life on Mars.

Glossary

Apollo 11 The whole spacecraft: the Command, Service and Lunar Modules.

biological isolation suit Germ-proof rubber body suit.

crater Huge hole on the Moon's surface.

desolation A lifeless, deserted place.

dock To link spacecraft together.

friction The rubbing together of one surface against another.

gravity The force which pulls everything to the ground.

laboratory A room or building where scientific experiments take place.

lunar Anything relating to the Moon.

module Word to describe one complete part of the spacecraft.

NASA National Aeronautical Space Administration based in Houston, Texas.

orbit The circling path around the Moon, the Earth or the Sun.

stage A section of a rocket.

vertical Upright.

USSR Union of Soviet Socialist Republics.